GAWAIN AND THE GREEN KNIGHT

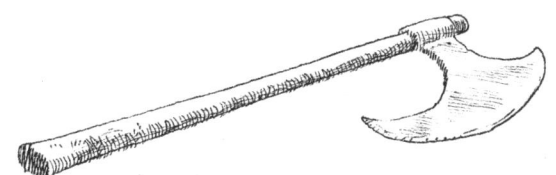

Original story by the Pearl Poet
Retold and illustrated by Philip Reeve
Series Advisor Professor Kimberley Reynolds

OXFORD
UNIVERSITY PRESS

Letter from the Author

I grew up in Brighton in the 1970s, where I spent a lot of my time writing, drawing and reading. After school I became an illustrator, but I always wanted to write stories as well as illustrate them, so eventually I became a writer too.

Somewhere along the way I fell in love with the legends of King Arthur, a wonderful collection of stories with their roots deep in the myths of Ancient Britain. *Gawain and the Green Knight* is one of them. It was written as a poem in the fourteenth century. The writer's name is forgotten but he also wrote another famous poem called *Pearl* – that's why he is sometimes called the 'Pearl Poet'. His poem about Gawain was lost for hundreds of years, but luckily one copy survived. It's a story about strange magic, a winter journey, and a very dangerous game. I've retold the story in my own words. I hope the Pearl Poet would approve ... and I hope you enjoy it!

Philip Reeve

Chapter One

Christmastime at Camelot. Snow crowned the towers and battlements. The wide moat lay white and still in the twilight, frozen hard enough to walk on. It did not matter, though, for the land was all at peace.

Only the snowflakes laid siege to King Arthur's castle, patting at its painted shutters, but no one heard them, for inside the Great Hall there was laughter and music. Arthur and his knights were feasting, as they had feasted each night of this Christmas season. Their appetites were huge after days in the saddle, jousting in the tourney-yard or hunting in the wintered woods. Up from the kitchens the servants brought a banquet: capons and venison, peacocks and partridges. Gold goblets were filled, and the songs of the minstrels rang among the roof beams.

The knights and their ladies all looked to Arthur, who sat at his high seat, with Queen Guinevere beside him. They waited for him to begin, for none of them could eat before their King did. But Arthur seemed thoughtful. He pushed away his plate, stood up, and raised his voice so all could hear him.

'Knights,' he said, 'the New Year is just beginning. Tonight I will not eat until I have heard some tale or seen some feat of chivalry and high adventure.'

'Hurrah!' the knights roared, a bit regretfully, looking at their heaped plates and brimming goblets, and hoping that somebody would have a tale to tell and tell it quickly.

There was usually no shortage of good tales at Camelot. The place was like a hive. All summer long the knights buzzed out of it to seek adventure, and brought back stories to be stored like honey and served up golden on dark winter evenings. But many tales had been told already that Christmastide, and now the knights looked at one another in dismay, realizing that they had no new ones to tell.

'Perhaps the King would like to hear again the story of Geraint and Enid?' said Sir Agravaine.

'Or maybe,' said Sir Bors, 'His Majesty would tell us again how he became King! How only he could pull the sword from the stone?'

But Arthur shook his head. Old tales are always welcome when friends gather, passing the familiar pieces of the past between them, but on this New Year's Night he felt a new story was needed.

And as he stood there, silent, pondering, there came a sound of hoofbeats from outside, and with a crash the great doors were flung wide. There was a flurry of snowflakes, and the cold night air made the candle flames flutter. Into Arthur's hall rode a horseman.

Knights leaped to their feet. They stared and shouted. Some reached for swords, remembered that they were not wearing them, and snatched butter knives instead, all ready to defend their King.

Servants hurried aside as the newcomer's horse clattered to the centre of the hall and reared up, raking the air with its hooves. The horse was huge, and the rider matched it. He was a giant of a man, and he was green. *Green!* The word ran through the hall as knights and ladies noticed. This was no trick of the light.

'He's green! All green!'

It was not just the stranger's clothes that startled them – his holly-green armour and his pine-green cloak, his grass-green breeches and his moss-green boots. His thick bushy hair was green too, and so was his broad beard. His face was as green as new leaves in springtime.

The trappings of his horse were green-on-green, and the hair of its coat was green, and the tangles of its mane and tail were pale grey-green, like the lichen-flags which wave from winter trees. The blade of the enormous axe in the rider's right hand gleamed with a light as green as sunshine in a summer wood.

This Green Knight grinned, baring teeth as green as young acorns. 'Who is the boss of this gang?' he demanded.

'I am,' said Arthur. 'And you are welcome to my hall.'

The stranger looked hard at him, and in his eyes the green light deepened, as the light on a green hill deepens when the shadow of a cloud sweeps over it.

'So you're King Arthur, are you? You've made quite a name for yourself, I'll say that for you. Wherever I go I hear folk singing your praises. And your knights are the finest fighters in all this land, I'm told. That's what brings me here. I thought I'd see for myself how brave they really are.'

Lamplight winked off the mighty axe he held. All around the hall, men stiffened and grew stern, hissing at their squires to fetch swords, shields and armour.

King Arthur said, 'If you come looking for battle, stranger, you will find it.'

But the Green Knight laughed. 'Nay!' he said, and held up his other hand, in which he grasped a branch of holly.

'This green bough shows I come in peace. A game is all I'm looking for. A pleasant pastime on a winter's night.

I have come here to challenge one of these knights of yours to a friendly competition. A simple test of strength and skill.'

He threw the branch down on the floor at Arthur's feet, and held up the axe.

'The rules are simple,' the Green Knight said. 'One of your men must trade me blow for blow. He shall take this axe I hold, and strike one blow at me, while I stand here stock still. And then I shall strike one blow at him. Does that sound fair?'

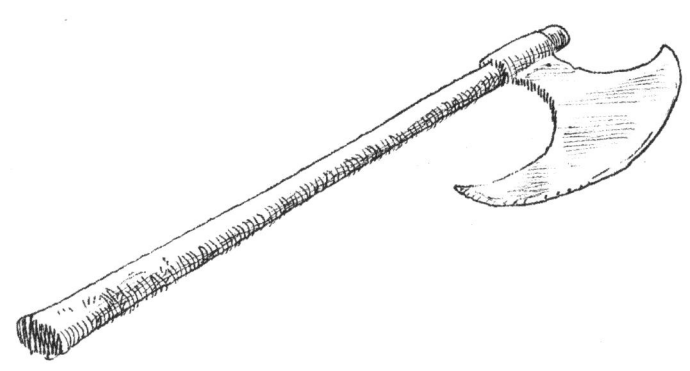

The Green Knight beamed round at the knights, holding out the axe, eager for someone to take it and hack at him. 'Come, who will have a bash? You can take the first swing!'

But the knights, who had been ready to fight him a moment ago, now hung back warily. They sensed a trick. They had all heard tales about the spells of the faerie folk who haunted the woods and waters of the wild. Where had he sprung from, this Green Knight, coming in twilight at the year's cold turning? What spells had called him forth from deep in some forest or beneath the hollow hills? The knights were brave men, bold in battle, but no man can fight magic.

'What?' said the Green Knight. 'Is this

truly Arthur's hall? Are you really his knights, who people tell such stories of? Won't one of you dare strike me? Are you all such craven cowards?'

Then one voice rang out. 'Give me your axe, green man!'

It was Gawain, Arthur's nephew, and the youngest of his knights, come newly to Camelot from his home in the north. A big lad, and handsome, his shoulders broad, his hair red-golden. He had arrived too late to fight in Arthur's wars. He had triumphed in tournaments, but he was untried in battle, and that made him shy, because his fellow knights were all brave warriors with high deeds behind them. He knew that he only had his place at Camelot because he was the King's nephew.

Now he saw a chance to earn his seat among the fellowship. He guessed this Green Knight had some trick up his green sleeve, but he thought he was clever enough to outwit him. So he left his bench and came between the tables, holding out his hand to grasp the green haft of the axe.

Then the Green Knight jumped down from his horse and stood in front of Gawain, arms folded, feet apart, awaiting the blow with a friendly green grin.

'Come on, then, lad! Strike me! We've not got all night!'

Gawain hefted the axe. A well-wrought weapon, beautifully balanced. Light rippled down the blade's bright edge like green water.

'One go,' the Green Knight said. 'That's all you get. And then I'll have my turn. Is that fair?'

'That is fair,' said Gawain. 'But I warn you, sir, no man I strike with this axe will ever be able to return the blow.'

'Well, I'll take that chance,' the Green Knight said, and closed his green eyes, ready for the blade.

Gawain gripped the axe haft and planted his feet wide. He swung back the axe, testing its weight, ready for the Green Knight to dodge when he struck. But the Green Knight stood as still as some tree in a clearing, smiling serenely as the axe swished towards him.

The blade bit through flesh and bone, clean through his neck.

The head of the Green Knight tumbled from his shoulders and rolled on the floor, while squires and servants scurried out of its way.

Gawain stepped back, breathless, glad of his victory, thrilled by the way the knights shouted his name, and the light in the eyes of the ladies who watched him. He stood holding the axe, waiting for the corpse of the Green Knight to collapse. But there it stood, arms folded, the blood falling red as holly berries on the shoulders of the green cloak.

Cabal, Arthur's hound, who waited out mealtimes beneath the King's table, stood up and went to where the severed head lay and sniffed at it – then leaped back with a yelp as the green eyes opened wide and the green teeth grinned at her.

'Nice work, lad!' said the head. 'That stung a bit!'

The headless body walked over and picked up the head by the hair. Held it up like a lantern and swung it this way and that so that it could see everyone in the hall. Knights muttered their prayers and ladies fainted. Queen Guinevere was horrified, King Arthur astonished. The green face wore a happy smile, as if the Green Knight were delighted at all the consternation he had caused.

He set his head back on his neck and shook it a few times to make sure that it was properly attached. Then he sauntered back to where poor Gawain stood waiting.

'Now, young Gawain,' he said, 'remember your promise, which you made to me just now in the presence of your King and all these good people.' And he held out his hand for the axe.

Gawain gulped. He nodded. He bowed. He handed over the axe. What else could he do? He was a knight of King Arthur, and knights never break their promises.

The Green Knight stepped back, swinging the axe. The blade made sharp sounds, shining with lamplight as it sliced the air. Gawain stood his ground and tried not to tremble, awaiting the blow he had promised to take.

Then the Green Knight lowered the axe. 'Nay, lad,' he laughed, 'there's no hurry. I'll grant you a year. Next New Year's Day you shall come and find me at my Green Chapel, and there I'll give you a nimble knock in exchange for the blow you just dealt me.'

Turning, he mounted his green horse again. He glanced down at Gawain with a friendly wink. Then he kicked his heels into the horse's flanks, and the horse turned, and reared, and neighed, and went galloping from the hall, its hooves striking sparks of green fire from the flagstones.

And Gawain thought to himself, *A year: I have one single year left to live*. And for a moment he felt desperately afraid.

But then he thought, *A year is a long time. All manner of things might happen in a year.*

When he looked at it that way, his meeting at the Green Chapel began to feel as if it were an age away. And meanwhile, his wager with the Green Knight would be the talk of Camelot; the knights and ladies of the court were talking of it already, all around him: 'Did you see the way young Gawain swung that axe?', 'How he hewed his head off with one blow?', 'And when the head spoke, and he picked it up ... '

Arthur was eating now, and the talk flowed, and toasts were drunk to Gawain's bravery, and he sat at the King's side that night and felt dizzy with the strangeness that he had seen, and flattered at his new fame.

But in the quieter moments, when the laughter and the talking lulled, in the gaps between the minstrels' songs, Gawain would think of the wintry woods outside, the wild hills waiting for him, and the quest that he would have to make before Christmas came again.

Chapter Two

A year is a long time to a young man. All through that spring Gawain was able to push thoughts of his coming quest into the corners of his mind. He was busy with better things: the travels of Arthur's court; the tournaments and feasts.

Easter came. On every hedge bank bobbed bright daffodils, trumpeting the joy of the returning spring into the sharp March wind. New life stirred in nest and bud, and death seemed like a dream. The Green Knight seemed like a dream, too; half-remembered, hard to believe in now that the dark nights were over and bright sunshine lit the land. Except that Gawain noticed people treating him with a careful kindness, and girls gazing at him with a sadness in their smiles, as if they knew that he would not be there when Easter came again.

Summer was next. The wheat in the long fields ripened as golden as Gawain's own hair, and the green shadows in the woods began to remind him of what lay ahead. He woke in the warm nights from dreams of the Green Knight sharpening his axe. Then harvest time, when the cruel scythes flashed, and the songs of the mowers rang across the hillsides, and wagons heaped with grain heaved their way to mill and granary. The berries reddened on the brambles, the leaves began to turn, and Gawain knew that it would soon be time to leave.

He lingered as long as he could. He did not want to say goodbye to Camelot.

He could not believe that three seasons had sped by so fast and winter would soon return. But there was no denying it. Flocks of falling leaves flew down, red and brown, to settle on the waters of the moat. One morning the fields around the castle were white with frost.

On the day after the Feast of All Souls, Gawain went to his uncle, King Arthur.

'My Lord,' he said, 'you know the promise that I made. Now the time has come when I must keep it. I must ride north to find the Green Chapel, and meet whatever doom awaits me there.'

Then King Arthur was filled

with sadness. It felt so unfair that this fine young man, at the start of his life, should go seeking his death. But death was better than dishonour, and Gawain would be dishonoured forever if he broke the oath that he had made. So Arthur nodded, and laid his hand on his nephew's shoulder, and prayed for him.

Then he called for the gift that he had prepared for Gawain: a new suit of armour from the royal armourer. A red carpet was spread upon the floor, and the gleaming gear laid out on it for Gawain to put on. Steel shoes in segments, like giant, shiny woodlice. Bright greaves and cuisses to armour his legs. A coat of steel

rings stitched over costly quilting. Armlets and gauntlets; bright metal; tough leather.

Dressed in it, Gawain felt splendid; braver already. It fitted so perfectly, was hinged so carefully, that it seemed to weigh nothing as he walked outside to where his horse waited. His white mare Gringolet tossed her head when he drew near, glad to see him and joyful at the thought of a journey, not knowing as he did where their road would lead them.

All Camelot seemed to have come out to watch as Gawain climbed into the saddle. Knights gathered round him, wishing him good luck. Ladies leaned from the windows, scullions peered from the kitchen doorways. All thinking how sad it was that such a brave and bright young man must ride away and be killed just because of a rash promise; a Christmas game!

But Gawain had promised himself that he would show no sadness. He settled himself in the saddle, and King Arthur handed up his new shield, which was red, and bore in gold a five-pointed star: the pentangle, or Endless Knot, the symbol of purity and truth. Gawain thanked the King. He slung the shield on his back by its stout straps. He raised his hand in farewell, and then, before anyone could make sad speeches, he kicked Gringolet's flanks and she trotted out of the courtyard, through the high gates, across the drawbridge.

The people of the surrounding country had all come out to see him set off. They lined the road outside Camelot as he cantered past them and away.

Past the fallow fields he rode, over the commons, a lonely traveller under a low grey sky. A wind from the north blew cold on his face, and as he crested the hill beyond Camelot, winter came to greet him, flinging handfuls of hail.

And so Gawain went on his way, with no clear notion where he was bound, and only a name to lead him there. Wherever he stopped on his journey, at the castles of friendly lords or the thatched huts of poor folk, he asked the same question: 'Have you heard of a place called the Green Chapel? For I must meet the Green Knight there, on New Year's Day.' No one knew of it. No one had heard of the Green Knight or his Chapel.

So Gawain rode on, while winter deepened and the roads grew worse. Soon there were no houses to stay at, rich or poor. He lit his fires in lonely places and saw the fire-glow flicker in the eyes of the wolves that watched him from the woods. He slept wrapped in his cloak, and woke sometimes to find it had grown a coat of cold white fur in the night.

The road led always upward, barely a road at all any more, just a track, a scar, a stream-bed along which poor Gringolet waded knee-deep.

This was the wild north country. Even the words were different here, so far from Camelot. The fierce, tumbling streams were called becks, or ghylls. The hills were fells, and the cold lakes lying cruel as mirrors in their hollows were called tarns. Wet bracken lay purple on the steep fellsides, and the frosted paths wandered whitely through it towards places steeper still. Sharp summits scratched at the sky and the clouds bled snow.

There among the knuckled crags wild men made their lairs. They hurled down stones on Gawain as he skirted the scree slopes; shards bounced from his shield and rang on his armour. He drew his sword and shouted challenges: 'Come out and fight me, you cowards!' But the wild men just hooted; fair fights were not their way. Their shouts rang from the rock faces. They threw down more stones, seeking to stun him. A sharp slate struck his saddle, and sliced through the strap of a satchel where most of his supplies were stowed. His food and possessions were strewn on the screes, and the wild men squabbled over the spoils while Gawain's scared horse took off at a gallop.

Wild men weren't the worst that those hills had to show him. Worms writhed from the waters; wolves howled on the heights. Giants harried Gawain over the high tops, shambling and roaring.

He found his way down from their country by sheep tracks, guiding Gringolet gingerly over the ice-slick stones. On the far side of the fells lay a forest, ancient and wild, a maze of ragged moss and twisting trees. There Gawain wandered, bewildered, wondering if there really was such a place as this Green Chapel, or whether it had just been the Green Knight's joke; a trick to lure him here to his lonely death among the crowding trees.

One day, dusk falling, the sky growing dim above the cage of bare branches, Gawain finished the last of the food he carried. There was nothing to hunt in that empty wood, no fodder for Gringolet, who stumbled down the winding paths, with her head hanging, whinnying in fear at the cry of the wolves.

Gawain sheltered from the falling snow under the boughs of a huge old oak. He thought maybe he had passed that oak already, yesterday or the day before. Maybe he was so lost that he was going around in circles, and would never find his way out of this treacherous tangle of trees. Shivering with the cold, he prayed for some

shelter, some place he could sleep safe and warm.

And then, through gathering darkness and the trunks of the trees, he saw a light flicker. It was not the light of a star, cold and far-off, but a golden light, and near at hand. The glow of a lighted window on a winter's night, which is the homeliest sight in the whole world.

Gawain patted Gringolet's neck. 'Come on girl,' he shouted, urging her forward. With the last of her strength the poor horse carried him through the twilight, and suddenly the trees thinned and fell behind, and there ahead a castle stood. It shone in the last light of the dreary day like a castle cut from paper; the hard-hewn stone of its walls washed white, and white chimneys trickling pale smoke into the sky. Its towers were lidded with thick snow,

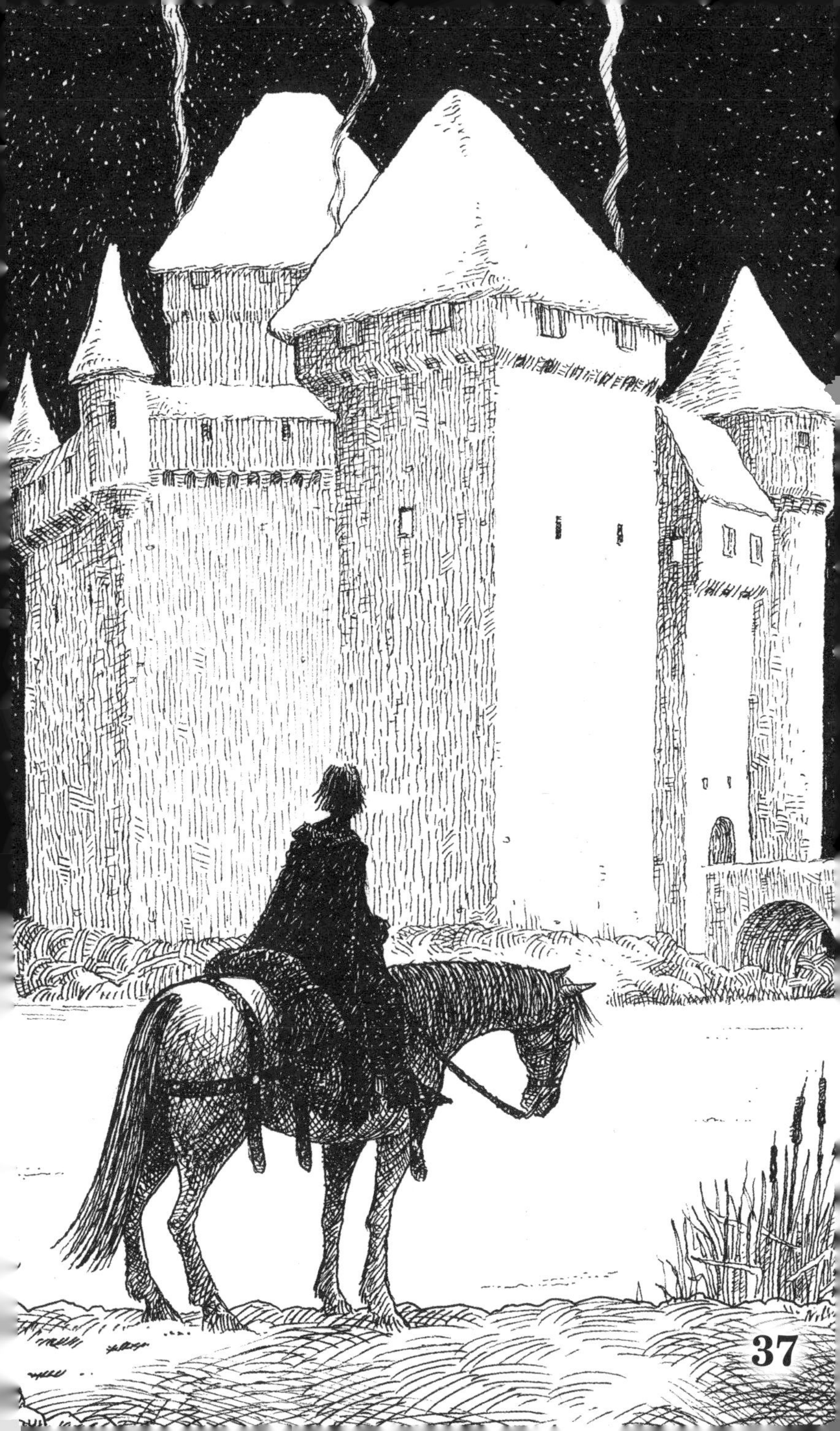

its drawbridge was drawn up, but from a window high in the gatehouse shone that welcoming light.

Gawain reined in Gringolet on the moat's edge and shouted across. No words in that shout, for his lips were too frosty to form them. It sounded like the cry of some wild beast, echoing from the panes of ice that paved the moat. But he shouted again, and a shutter opened, the face of a porter peering out at him.

'Good sir,' Gawain managed to say, 'I seek shelter. Will you carry a message to the master of this house and ask if I may stay overnight here?'

'By all that's holy,' laughed the porter, 'I'll go right away, and you may be sure he'll welcome you.'

Then the shutter closed again, and Gawain

sat alone on his horse at the moat's edge, shuddering with cold, until with a clang and a groan and a rattle the drawbridge descended, and out from the castle came servants and squires sent to welcome him in.

As if in a dream, Gawain let them lead him, Gringolet's tired hooves clip-clopping over the long bridge. In a torchlit courtyard he eased himself stiffly from his saddle and stood stretching while stable boys led his horse away.

Then, across the courtyard, a big voice came booming, 'Welcome!' and a big man followed it, beaming, spreading his arms wide, wrapping Gawain in a welcoming hug.

'I am Sir Bertilak, lord of this place. Welcome, traveller! Not many come riding over the high fells so late in the year, but we are glad to see you, and here you'll stay a while, I hope, to pass Christmas in peace and rest from your roving!'

'Christmas?' said Gawain.

'Aye!' said Sir Bertilak, beaming more broadly. 'You have come to us on Christmas Eve.'

Gawain had not realized how long he had wandered in the wilds. He knew that he could not stay with this good knight. Within a few days he must keep his meeting at the Green Chapel, wherever that might be.

But it was so good to hear friendly voices round him, and to catch from a kitchen window the smell of roasting game, that

he could not bring himself
to leave.

And anyway, he thought, *poor Gringolet needs food and care, and so do I. One day's rest can do no harm. I shall keep Christmas in this kindly place and ride on stronger afterward ...*

Then Gawain looked down at his raggedy cloak and rusting armour, and ran a hand through the knots of his hair, and felt ashamed. But Sir Bertilak just laughed again and said, 'Now then, let my servants tend to you, before you come to meet our company.'

And so they took Gawain up winding stairs to a high chamber, where the walls were prettily painted and hung with rich tapestries, where a fire danced and crackled in the big hearth. Some filled a bath, scattering dried rose petals on the water, while others helped Gawain out of his grimy gear. And when he was washed, and shaved, and looked like a human being again, they brought him rich robes to wear, fresh linen crisp against his tingling clean skin.

In the great hall of the castle a feast was laid out, with food that looked as fine to Gawain as any that he had eaten at King Arthur's court – finer, perhaps, for at Camelot he had never been quite so hungry.

Sir Bertilak made him sit at his side, at the high table, and asked him many questions as he ate. For it seemed the stories of Arthur and the great deeds of his knights had reached even that wild north country, and Sir Bertilak and his men were eager to hear the truth of them, and very pleased to have beneath their castle's roof one of Arthur's famous knights.

Everyone listened as Gawain told them of his journey, and the strange quest, which had brought him north in the dying of the year. And none listened more raptly than Sir Bertilak's wife, who sat upon his other side, and who Gawain thought was the loveliest lady he had ever seen, more beautiful even than Queen Guinevere herself. She gasped as he told of his vow to the Green Knight, and her grey eyes grew wide when he spoke of his skirmishes with wild men and ogres, until he began to feel as if he was telling his tale for her alone. But at last he remembered himself, and said to Sir Bertilak, 'So I am sorry to say that I may not linger here, sir. I must ride on my way tomorrow.'

His host seemed crestfallen. 'What? Leave us so soon? Why?'

'Because on New Year's Day I have vowed to be at a place called the Green Chapel, and I still have no notion of where it lies, nor how I am to find it.'

Then Sir Bertilak, who seldom stopped laughing for long, laughed loudly again. 'The Green Chapel?' he said. 'Why, you have almost found it!

It is in the fells, but two miles or so from my door – a pleasant morning's ride! Your journey is ended, Sir Gawain. Stay here this Christmastime, and when the New Year dawns, one of my men will lead you to the place.'

Chapter Three

Gawain slept that night in a bed as soft as summer clouds, and if dreams of his journey or the Green Knight troubled him, he did not remember them when he woke. The sun was high, the fresh snow shone, the world was glittering, and it was Christmas morning.

All through that day and the next, and the next, there was feasting and joyfulness in the castle of Sir Bertilak. Branches of greenery hung from the roof beams, and under them everyone laughed and made merry. Drummers and pipers made music to dance to, old songs were sung and old stories unfolded.

At dinner Gawain sat beside Bertilak's wife, who was eager to hear all that he could tell her of his life in Camelot and the ways of the court there. Even if she had not been so beautiful, Gawain would still have loved her, for she was wise, and kind, and her laughter and stories made him almost forget the sharp edge of the axe blade that waited for him at the year's turning.

One night as Sir Gawain started upstairs to his chamber, Sir Bertilak came to him, smiling as always.

'Tomorrow we ride out with the hounds. The hunting in my woods is as good as any you'd enjoy on the deer paths of King Arthur's forests ... '

Then Sir Bertilak stopped. Perhaps he had seen the way Gawain's face fell, the way his shoulders sagged at the thought of having to leave the comfort and warmth of the castle and go out into the cold hills again. He slapped Gawain on the back, and said, 'Nay, lad, I'm forgetting. You've a hard road behind you, and a strange one ahead. Rest is what you need. You'll want your strength and your wits with you when you go to meet the Green Knight. So you stay here tomorrow, and do whatever you wish. My wife will keep you company and I shall see you when I ride home at sundown.'

Gawain said his thanks, and was about to turn away, when Sir Bertilak added, 'And I have an idea. Just in case you mind missing the sport, I'll make you a wager. Whatever I win in the woods I'll give to you. And whatever you win here while I'm gone, you'll give to me in exchange. Is that fair?'

Gawain thought Sir Bertilak was joking. What could he hope to win, tucked up snug in his bed, or sitting at a table? So he laughed and agreed, and went on his way, back to his chamber where his warm bed waited.

A few hours later, when dawn was faintly silvering the cracks of sky around his shutters, Gawain half-heard the hooves of the hunters' horses drumming on the drawbridge, the belling of the hounds, and the hunting horns calling, away in the woods. And he felt very glad that he was not out there with them in the frost, and turned over and went back to sleep.

Out in the sunrise the hounds flowed like water over the feet of the fells. Their baying filled the air like peals of Christmas bells, echoing among the wooded crags, setting the deep dales ringing. Deer broke from their cover in the deep thickets. White tails flashing, they fled through the trees.

Sir Bertilak let the harts pass. But beaters turned the hinds back, yelling 'Let!' and 'Ware!', driving them into a cleft of the hillside. There the hunters dropped from their saddles and took up their bows, loosing arrows which sped through the trees and bit deep into deer flesh. The beasts fell, thrashing and bleeding. Those that broke from the combe were harried by hounds, or by hunters who hared after them, with Sir Bertilak in the lead, laughing, filled with love of the hunt and the wild woods around him, his bow in his hand and his big horn booming.

The horn-calls echoing off the crags woke brave Gawain where he lay in his bed. Slim shafts of sunlight reached in through the shutters and fingered his bed curtains. He lay there pleasantly numb, thinking about getting up, until suddenly he heard the door of the chamber open. Someone was moving around outside the bed's closed curtains. A servant, he thought, come to tidy and clean, until, through a gap in them he saw that it was Sir Bertilak's wife. He closed his eyes, and pretended to sleep, but after a moment she twitched open the curtains and sat down beside him on the edge of the bed.

'Good morning, Sir Gawain,' she said. 'Not still asleep, surely? Is this how late they lie in bed at Camelot?'

53

'My lady,' said Gawain, pretending to wake. 'What brings you here?'

'Why, you do,' said Sir Bertilak's wife. 'It is not every day that a brave and famous knight comes riding to us through the high hills, all the wild way from Camelot, and I want to make the most of your visit. My husband and his men are all out at the hunt, my ladies are busy, the servants too; I am lonely and I want to hear more of your stories. So I have come to lay siege to you here, until you tell them. You cannot escape; I have bolted the door, so no one can disturb us.'

'But I have told you all the tales I know,' said Gawain. 'And I am not really such a brave and noble knight; I'm no one really, the least of all the knights of Camelot.'

'Then tell me about the others,' said the lady, laughing. And so he did, talking and talking while she sat and listened, watching him always. And at last, when he could think of no more, she said, 'Perhaps what you say is true, and you are not brave or noble.'

'Why?' asked Gawain, who had not really meant that bit.

She blushed. 'Because I should think that a knight who

was brave and noble would at least offer a kiss to a lady. It is only polite. Perhaps you are not really one of Arthur's knights at all, but just a wanderer who has spun a tale about himself.'

'Well, if a kiss is what you want, then you shall have it,' said Gawain. And she wrapped her arms around him and pulled him close to her and kissed him, and then sat back, and smiled, and said, 'There! Now I have what I longed for and I shall leave you in peace, for this day, at least.'

And when she had gone, Gawain got up and dressed and went downstairs into the hall, where a meal was being made ready for the hunters, who would soon be riding home.

The moon was up by then, a new nail-paring, snagged like a fish-hook in the trees on the crags. Through the twilight Sir Bertilak and his men rode home, the breath of their weary horses smouldering on the cold air, men on foot beside them lugging the carcasses of all the deer they'd killed, the muzzles of the hounds red where they had feasted on the guts and entrails.

Across the drawbridge they clattered, into the yard, and Gawain came out with everyone else to see the dead deer heaped up there.

'A good day's hunting!' roared Sir Bertilak, jumping from his horse and waving at the mountain of meat. 'And I've not forgotten our wager, Gawain; all this is yours.'

'It's a fine haul,' said Gawain. 'Not even Arthur himself has killed so many in a single day.'

'And how did your hunting go?' said Sir Bertilak. 'What did you win, inside these walls of mine?'

Gawain thought for a moment. 'Only one thing,' he said, and he put his arms around Sir Bertilak's neck and kissed him.

Sir Bertilak jumped back, surprised. Then he began to laugh. 'I'd like to know where in my house you found such a prize!'

'That wasn't part of our bargain, my lord,' said Gawain. 'I said I'd give you what was given me, no more, and that I've done.'

'Fair's fair!' agreed Sir Bertilak. 'Tomorrow I'll ride out again, and if you like, we'll make the same wager again.'

Gawain agreed; there seemed no harm in the game, and he saw how much it amused his host. So they shook hands on it, and went in together to the hall, where their supper waited.

And so, the next day, things took the selfsame course. Soon after sunrise the fells roared and rang with the echoes of the hounds. In the depths of the woods they found a scent that wound like a red thread around thickets and boulders. It led them to a brindled boar, a massive beast, scarred by the spears of hunters he'd foiled in other winters.

They flushed him from his lair among the mossy rocks, and chased him along the shores of a frozen tarn and up the fellside at a place where a stream came down in sour-milk-coloured waterfalls over rocks bearded with icicles. Cornered among the crags, the monster turned at bay, driving his sharp tusks at the hounds that harried him, flinging dogs into the air, hurling them maimed and howling down the hillside.

Then Sir Bertilak, leaping from the saddle, snatched a great boar-spear from his squire and started up the hill into the thick of the fight. And the old boar flung itself at him, coming down on him like a landslide with its mad black eyes a-glitter, Sir Bertilak crouching to meet its charge, jamming the butt of the boar-spear into the thin felltop turf.

While back in the castle, Gawain slept

in soft sheets, and woke to hear the lady of the place let herself into his chamber; the snick of the latch as she shut the door, the snap of the bolt as she barred it. He had been afraid she'd come. He had been hoping she would come. He sat up as she twitched the curtains open.

'Now, Sir Gawain,' she said, 'I hope I do not have to remind you of the lesson in politeness which I taught you yesterday.' And she put her arms around him and let him kiss her, just once.

Then they sat as they had sat before, snug in the tent of the curtained bed, and talked of tales they'd heard and things they'd seen, of Gawain's home, and the lady's, till the sky outside took on the dusty, dusky, duck-egg blue of evening. Then she kissed him again, and left him, and just as Gawain had the day before, he dressed and descended to the hall, in time to see Sir Bertilak and his party come clattering into the yard.

Sir Bertilak's clothes were all drenched in black blood, so that people feared he was wounded. But when he saw Gawain he let out a laugh, and swung down from his saddle the head of the boar; massive, mad-eyed, scarred by hounds' teeth, yellow tusks gleaming, red tongue lolling. He let it fall on the flagstones at Gawain's feet. 'There!' he said. 'Did you ever see such a beast before, Sir Gawain?'

Gawain shook his head. 'Not even Arthur has slain such a

boar, that I have heard of.'

Then Sir Bertilak laughed again, delighted. 'I'll give you its head, Gawain, in honour of our agreement,' he said. 'Now let us see what you have caught today.'

Gawain hesitated for a moment. Then he hugged the old knight, and placed his hands upon his bearded cheeks, and kissed him sweetly: once; twice.

Sir Bertilak raised one shaggy eyebrow at the first kiss, another at the second. 'Well,' he said, 'you have done better than yesterday. Twice as well, in fact. But let us see how you fare tomorrow. Shall we make the same wager once more?'

Gawain agreed, and then realized that tomorrow's game would be the last. For tomorrow was New Year's Eve, and on the morning after he must leave this castle and his kindly host and go to seek the Green Knight at his chapel.

That night, despite the softness of the sheets and the snugness of the bedchamber, Gawain did not sleep soundly. Dark dreams kept coming to him, in which the Green Knight waited, headless and horrible, heaving up his axe, swinging it down, landing the blow which Gawain had promised he would bear without flinching.

Then into his dreams came a shaft of daylight, and the voice of the lady saying, 'Sweet Gawain, how can you sleep so deep and snore so loud when the sun is up and the morning almost done?'

He opened his eyes. It was bright daytime; New Year's Eve; cold sunshine outside, and the horns of the hunt ringing from far-off fells. The lady of the castle was leaning over him, her face above him looking down. And this time he did not need to be told, but gently kissed her, once, and twice, and then a third time.

Then they sat and talked together, as they had sat the day before and the day before that, except that today Gawain knew this would be the last time he spoke with her; their time alone was running out. She looked very lovely, in her gown that left her shoulders bare, with those clustered pearls in her hair, and her cheeks red as rose petals, and her eyes sad and laughing. He would have liked to kiss her again, and he thought that she would like that too, but he knew that it would not be a knightly way to repay Sir Bertilak for his hospitality. So nothing passed between the two of them but fond words.

When it was time for the lady to leave she said, 'Gawain, my husband tells me that tomorrow you must depart. And I shall miss you so much.'

'And I shall miss you,' he said, truthfully.

'Is there some gift you could give me?' she asked. 'Some favour, however small, that will remind me of you?'

'I'm sorry,' said Gawain. 'I have nothing to give you. I came here alone, looking only for death, a wanderer in an unknown land, and I brought no bags of precious stones or beautiful gifts with me. If I had, they should all be yours.'

'Then I shall just take my memories of these pleasant days,' the lady said, 'and keep them in my heart, like treasure. And in return, let me give you a gift, Gawain.'

She unclasped her belt, a girdle of green silk hemmed with gold, and drew it from around her waist. 'This was a gift to me,' she said, 'from my aunt, the sorceress

Morgan le Fay. It is supposed to protect the wearer from all harm.'

Gawain, who had been about to tell her that he could not accept her gift as he had nothing to give her in return, paused when he heard that. He recalled the dark dreams which had plagued him in the night, and a shameful, unknightly thought crept into his mind.

'From all harm, you say?'

'Oh yes, Gawain. Anyone who buckles this belt tightly around him need fear no blow that is struck against him. The magic woven in it will deflect all blades.'

'Then I am glad of your gift, and I give you thanks for it,' said Gawain, and took it from her, and ran his thumbs over the fine-woven fabric, wondering. It would be a cowardly act to trust such magic in a fight against a human foe, but surely not against the Green Knight, who had magic of his own.

Fair's fair, thought Gawain, and when the lady left him he buckled the belt on under his tunic, hidden from everyone, and went down to make ready for the next day's journey, feeling for the first time a faint hope that he might live to see tomorrow night alive.

All through that day, while Gawain and the lady spoke of love, Sir Bertilak and his companions had been chasing a fox over high, bald hills and through tree-choked dales. The fox was old and wily; it had run through becks and bogs to throw the hounds off its scent; led them a long and merry chase.

70

But at last in the long light of the evening sun they caught the fox, flushed it from the thorn thicket where it had gone to ground. The hounds piled onto it, wailing like demons, tails thrashing, teeth gnashing, until their lord waded among them, pulling them aside to lift the fox high, out of the reach of their jaws. Horns were sounded, and loud hurrahs; high echoes shivering among the crags; the rest of the hunters came riding up, those who'd been lost drawn to the sound of the kill.

Then the slain fox was skinned, and with horns still howling the hunters turned their horses' heads towards the white castle on the wood's edge, towards the warm lights of home.

In the great hall that night, in the midst of the New Year feasting, Sir Bertilak presented Gawain with the fox skin and said, 'Not even Arthur has been led such a chase, I'll bet, nor fetched home such a fine skin at the end of it. And how did your hunting go, Gawain?'

Then Gawain gently kissed him, three times.

And Sir Bertilak, after a moment, said, 'Three kisses? A better prize than a stinking fox fur, some might say. But are you quite sure no other prize came your way today? Anything you gained is mine, remember.'

Gawain thought of the belt he wore; the girdle woven from green and golden silk and helpful magic. He could feel it beneath his tunic for it was a tad too tight; the lady was more slender than him. If he was to honour the wager he had made, he should present it to Sir Bertilak – but then what hope would he have of surviving the Green Knight's axe-blow next morning?

'Nothing else,' he said. 'Those three kisses were the whole of my haul.'

For a moment Sir Bertilak looked as if he knew that Gawain was keeping something from him. Then a smile spread across his face again and he clapped an arm around the young man's shoulders and said, 'Come; tomorrow morning it will be New Year, and you must complete your quest to meet this green fellow. But tonight you are our guest still. You'll eat and drink your fill with us again, and hear in full the tale of how we found our fox.'

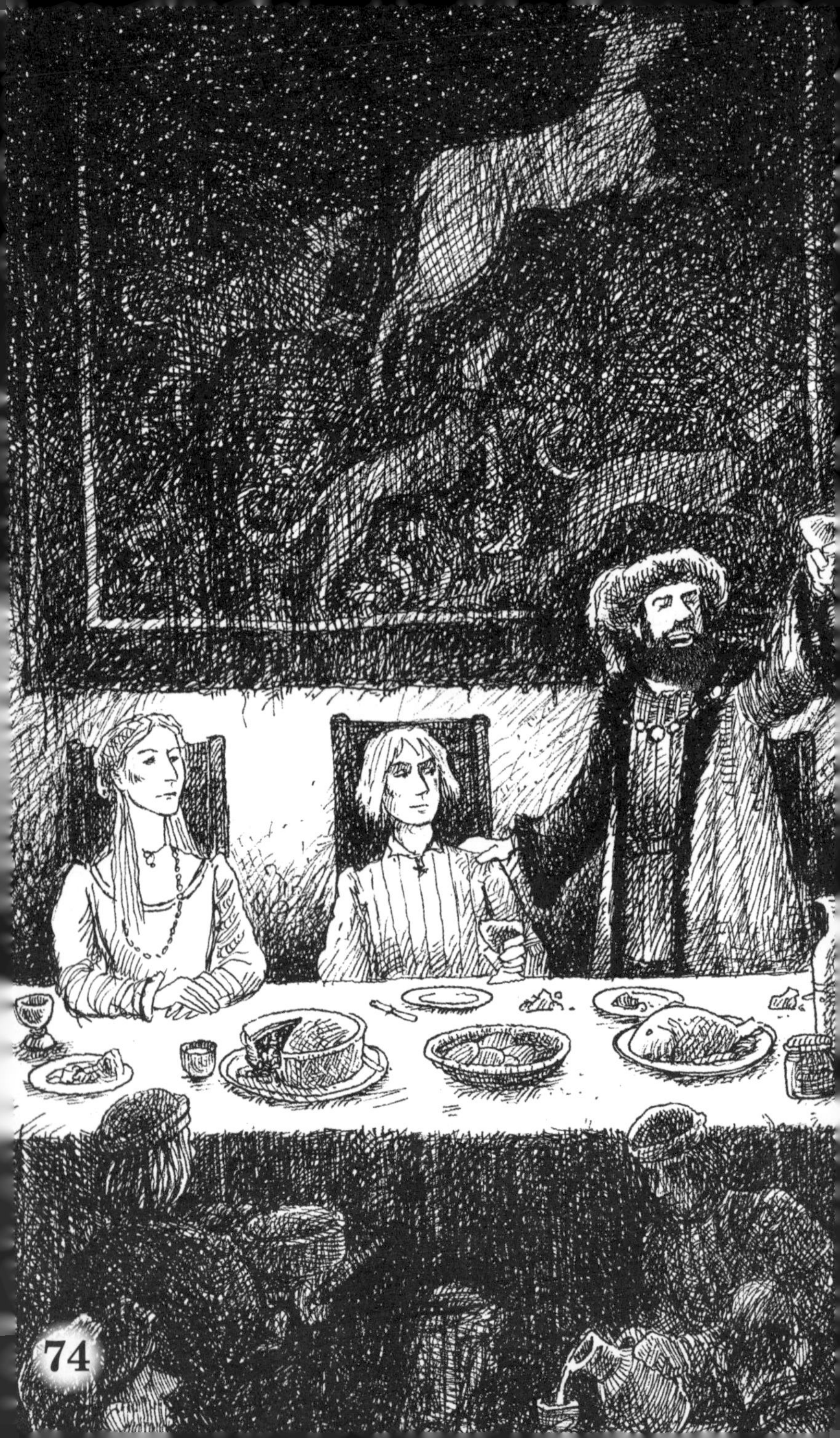

So Gawain ate and drank, and heard the story of the hunt, and afterwards he made his goodbyes and said his thank you to the kindly knight and the people of the castle, and especially to Sir Bertilak's wife, although with all the others crowded round about her there were many things that he wanted to tell her which had to stay unsaid.

Gawain slept dreamlessly that night. When he woke it was still dark, and it was not the gentle lady of the place who roused him, but a man Sir Bertilak had sent to guide him to the Green Chapel.

Chapter Four

No one was awake to watch him go. That was what Gawain had hoped for, as he remembered his leave-taking at Camelot, and knew that partings are painful. Dressed in his armour again, sat astride Gringolet, he followed his guide across the drawbridge, through the trees, up onto the empty fells. Flocks of small birds wheeled against the sunrise, settling in the snowy heather until the horses drew near, then scattering into the sky again to wheel and settle further on.

From the top of the first step Gawain looked back, hoping for a last glimpse of the white castle where he had been so happy, but it was gone, as if the woods had swallowed it. He could almost have believed that his stay there had been a dream, except that he was well fed, and Gringolet was fit again, and his armour was polished and his clothes freshly washed, and under his tunic the lady's green girdle clasped him tightly.

Gawain went on his way, following Sir Bertilak's servant over moors where the white woolly bellies of the clouds reached down to brush the grass. They forded fierce streams, which tumbled down out of the mountains, from the high black crags with their slashes of snow. A half-drowned sun lay low and watery on the eastern sky. The hooves of the horses made heartbeats on the cold peat.

Over three hills and three dales they rode, till they stopped on a height overlooking a wild, wooded place. There the servant said, 'Below us lies the place which Sir Bertilak told me to bring you to. But I beg of you sir, don't go down there. It's called the Green Chapel, but it ain't no church, and no gentle priest awaits you there. It's the lair of a wild man, a savage giant who lives for murder. If you go down there, Sir Gawain, you'll not return. No man, however brave, can hope to fight that monster and survive. I like you, young sir, and so I beg of you, don't go. No one will know that you failed in your quest; I'll not tell a soul. You can find your way by another road home to your own country, and I shall go back to Sir Bertilak and tell him with hand on heart that I brought you here, and that here we parted.'

'My thanks,' said Gawain. 'But I have come this far to keep my promise. I cannot break it now.'

The servant sadly shook his head, as if it made him sorry to see someone as young and brave as Gawain so set on throwing his life away. But he pointed downhill, where a path went winding through the heather, into a place where dwarfish oak trees clustered close among big boulders tumbled from the fells.

'There it lies,' the servant said. 'There you'll find the Green Chapel, and the ogre who haunts it. And now I'll bid you farewell, for I'll not go another step closer to that dreadful place.'

He tugged on his reins, pulling his

horse's head around. Kicking his heels into its flanks, he galloped away, hoofbeats fading into the sigh of the grass and the far frail calls of the curlews. Gawain watched him go, then started down alone into the valley.

He had expected a building of some sort; maybe in ruins, but at least a roof, a steeple, a few stony walls raised to the sky. There was nothing. Only the bare trees, lichen-draped, snow-speckled, and a river that roiled and rampaged through the valley bottom.

Down near the water stood a sort of low hill, too round to

be natural. A barrow perhaps, burial place of kings of old, whose names had faded into the wind. Great slabs of stone crowned it, shrugged from the fells' shoulders, propped up by luck or heaved into place by human hands, Gawain could not tell. There was a hole at one end, moss-green shadows within. He turned Gringolet towards it, and as she walked closer he heard above the river-roar another sound.

Chat, chat, chat ...

The call of some moorland bird? Or a thrush, maybe, hammering snail shells on its anvil of stone?

And then he drew near to the barrow's mouth, where the old stones shielded him from the water's noise, and he knew the sound for what it was; a sound he'd often heard in castle armouries and woodsmen's crofts, but had not expected in this lonely place.

It was the sound of a whetstone, sharpening a blade.

'This is no chapel,' said Gawain. 'It is nought but an old cave. And it has an evil feel. The sort of place where ghosts and spirits walk.'

Then he jumped down from Gringolet. He readied his shield and drew his sword. He scrambled over stones and tree roots to where the big boulders leaned, and pushed his way through the doorway they made.

There was no roof to the old barrow. Inside the space which the stones enclosed, thin shafts of wintry sun shone down through the branches of trees which had rooted themselves among the rocks. A carpet of last year's leaves lay underfoot, and at the far end, where a little stream came trilling down in shadows, the Green Knight sat sharpening his axe.

He glanced up when he heard Gawain, and bared his teeth in a green grin. Springing up nimbly, he came to greet his guest, saying, 'Heaven keep you, Gawain! Welcome to my hall! You've timed your travels well. Now let's finish this game we began. Take off your tin helmet and I'll repay that blow you dealt me at Arthur's place a twelvemonth back.'

84

Gawain took off his helmet and the padded cap which went beneath it. He shook out his hair, gold in the sunlight. He saw before him an old square stone, like a mossy table. He propped his sword and shield next to the stone and leaned over it, baring his neck to the green man's blade and doing his best not to look afraid.

Beneath his tunic Gawain could feel the magic belt cinched tight about his waist, but it seemed a silly thing next to the mighty axe the Green Knight wielded. How could a girdle save him from such sharpness?

The Green Knight grunted, raising the axe high, swinging it down with enough force to slice through flesh and blood and the bone beneath. Gawain flinched as it fell, and the blade swerved aside, bit deep into bare stone, scattering sparks.

'Oh, come on now, Sir Gawain,' the Green Knight chided, 'are you a man or a mouse? Or are you a snail, pulling your head back into your shell of armour when danger threatens? I thought Arthur's knights were made of better stuff!'

'Then strike again,' said Gawain. 'And

this time I'll not flinch.'

Nor did he. The axe went up; the axe came down, but just before the blade bit into Gawain's neck the green man stopped it, stepping back.

'That's better!' he said. 'Now you've pulled yourself together, I shall take you apart, as I promised.'

'Then hurry up,' said Gawain, tiring of the green man's tricks. 'Enough of your threats, you old green bully; strike, or let me go on my way!'

The Green Knight laughed. 'By heaven,' he said, 'I'll show you I mean business, Gawain; I'll split you like firewood.'

For the third time, the last time, the awful axe rose. The Green Knight growled as he swung it down. Its edge flashed fire, as sharp as any razor. But instead of sending Gawain's head spinning from his shoulders, the blow just cut his neck a little; the sort of wound men give themselves every day while they are shaving.

A flick of blood came from the gash and fell redly on the moss. Gawain sprang back a spear's length, snatching his sword and shield, shaking his hair from his eyes.

'Enough!' he shouted. 'One blow was our bargain. Three blows you have struck at me, and I've stood them each as promised. If you want to strike more, then I shall repay them, my sword against your hatchet.'

But the Green Knight did not charge at him. He just stood there laughing, leaning on his axe, and the steam of his hot breath hung in the sunbeams like dragon's smoke, and made a mist to hide him.

'Fearless Gawain! How fierce you sound! But put away your sword now. It was nowt but a game all along, and now it is over.'

And the mist cleared and it seemed to Gawain that the Green Knight had changed. He was as green as ever, but

Gawain knew him now; that loud laugh and kindly smile. The Green Knight was Sir Bertilak, and had been all along.

'That's right!' he roared, beaming at Gawain's bewilderment. 'Sir Bertilak is me, and I am he, and everything that happened at my castle was part of my game, Gawain. I've long wondered whether the knights of King Arthur could really be as brave and true as men make out, or whether the news I hear from Camelot is naught but stories. So I have tested you, Gawain, and my wife helped me. It was I who set her to come to your room while I hunted, and if you'd lied about what went on between you then my first blow would have slain you. But you were true to your word, and passed on her kisses to me two days running. That's why I struck and spared you twice; once for the first day and once for the second. Only on the third day did you play me false, and that's why my third blow nicked your neck. For you caught more than you let on that day, didn't you? Come now, let's be having it – my good wife's green girdle, which you wear round your waist.'

Ashamed, Gawain reached under his armour and took off the belt. He flung it at the Green Knight's feet as if it were a snake.

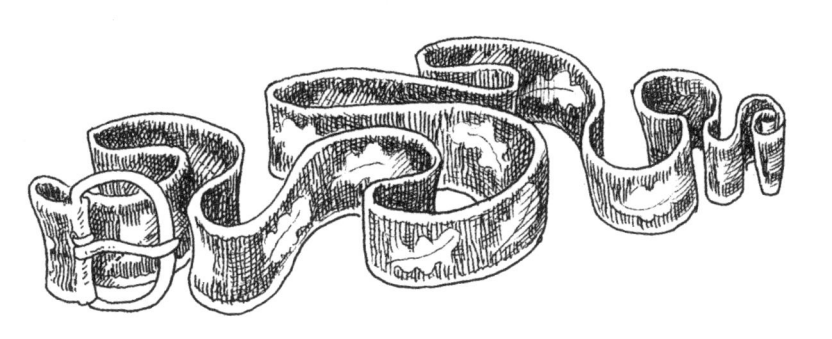

'So I have failed your test,' he said, 'and all for that. I wish I'd not accepted it, but she said it would keep me safe, and I was in such fear of my life that I took it. Now you know that I am a coward, and no doubt you'll think all Arthur's knights are as cowardly as me. But truly, none of them would have repaid your kindness and courtesy with such untruthfulness. Please let me know what I can do to make things right again.'

The Green Knight chuckled. He clapped his huge green hand on Gawain's shoulder. 'Nay, lad, you've confessed your wrongdoing, and I've spilled a thimbleful of your blood in return. All debts between the two of us are settled, and I have no doubt that you're the bravest of all Arthur's men. None of the others took up my challenge, after all. And who can blame you for loving your own life, and fearing death? Without fear to overcome, there'd be no point to bravery. So take back this girdle that's as green as me, and let it remind you of your adventures here when you are back in softer lands, mingling with gentler kinds of men. And now come, New Year is still young; ride back to my castle. My wife will be waiting; she did not like tricking you and will want to tell you how sorry she is.'

'Thank you,' said Gawain. But he knew that he would never return to Sir Bertilak's castle, and never again see the face of its lady, except in his dreams. 'My road lies south,' he said. 'I've lingered too long in these wilds. I must find my way home. Give my love to your wife, and my thanks, and my thanks to your people, who looked after me so well this Christmastide.'

'Then Heaven keep you, Gawain,' the Green Knight said. He tied the green girdle around Gawain's arm, knotted it tight over his armour to remind him of his adventures and the lessons he'd learned at the Green Chapel.

Then Gawain mounted Gringolet, and rode away. He glanced back once, and saw the Green Knight still standing at the entrance to his chapel with one green arm upraised to wave farewell.

But when he looked back again, from the edge of the woods, he could see nothing but trees, and the shadows of trees, and the moss shining emerald green in the sun.

Gawain laughed. He laughed for sheer joy at just being alive on that first day of the newborn year. And then he turned Gringolet's head towards the south and sought the steep roads that would lead him back through the hills, carrying his story home to Camelot.